All the Queens Gardens

I0799075

jovis

All the Queens Gardens

Everyday Landscaping in New York's Largest and Most Diverse Borough

Rafael Herrin-Ferri

jovis

6

A Queens Pastoral

Lynnette Widder

Spring in the Manhattan household of my childhood inevitably seemed to prompt a craving in my parents to return to their respective home boroughs. Spring meant we picnicked amongst jonquils in the Bronx Botanical Gardens, even if we had to eat my mother's sandwiches from gloved fingers. Spring meant we piled in the car to see azaleas blooming across Forest Hills Gardens, a trip my father always rewarded with ice cream at Jahn's. As much as I loved my Bronx grandmother for the chickens she'd raised in her World War II victory garden, Queens won me over. It wasn't only the ice cream. The milk I drank for breakfast came from Elmhurst, a dairy in Queens. The bread we ate—in my childhood, the spongy, fragrant stuff from Silvercup or Fink, and later, the fancier sourdough from Tom Cat or Amy's—came from Queens. Queens belonged historically on New York's kitchen tables. It had been the City's pantry from the late 18th century onwards. New York City's oldest tree, a tulip poplar estimated to be 350 years old, still stands in Queens as I write. Verdant, bucolic Queens has always loomed large in my imagination.

That Queens imaginary, its basis in an agrarian landscape replete with Jersey cows and cider orchards that once stretched from the banks of the East River to the coves of Jamaica Bay, persists in transfigured form, front yard by front yard and planter by planter, in the gardens that edge the borough's sidewalks, central courtyards, and rear alleys. Perhaps there is a correlation to be made between such passionate gardening and the fact that, according to municipal records, Queens has the City's largest number of foreign-born inhabitants. Regardless of antecedent, front and back yards throughout the borough are stylish and ingenious in equal measure. Episodic and idiosyncratic in and of themselves, the spaces, surfaces, and ensembles of All the Queens Gardens have been made coherent and comparable here through the typological categories into which the architect-author

Rafael Herrin-Ferri has empathetically placed them. At the intersection between an architectural study and an anthropological inventory, his collection encompasses as much evidence of skillful and determined caretaking as of humor, exuberance, and a crafty refusal to be undermined by New York's constrained land or seasonal givens.

Morning milk carton aside, though, it was industrial Queens that dominated the daily experience of my childhood. The skyline I saw across the river was punctuated by the "Big Allis" power plant, its enormous red and white painted smoke stacks rising like Cat-in-the-Hat legs above a cityscape of factory buildings and rail yards. Much later in life, at a gallery show, I discovered the Swiss photographer Rudy Burckhardt's shots of Queens from the 1940s. I recognized in those photos the place we'd traversed during family excursions to visit friends and relatives in the suburbs. That version of Queens hadn't changed much in the thirty years between Burckhardt's visits and my '70s childhood: an underpeopled cityscape in which small homes still stood alone on lots otherwise crossed by infrastructure; or in which spontaneous vegetation coexisted with front yards populated by fences, sculptures, stoops, trees, even a victory garden like the one my grandparents had tended in the other borough. Burckhardt's album presages the photos in this book, both in content and in methodologically precise comparison. Queens was, and remains, a both/and borough, its cultural landscape as much constructed as vegetative.

These two aspects, agrarian and industrial, have never been mutually exclusive. It was at Flushing Meadows, during the two Queens World's Fairs of 1939 and 1964, that the general public fell in love with early visions of leafy American suburbia, and later, lined up in a snail-shell-shaped pavilion to catch a glimpse of Michelangelo's Pietà, shipped over from the Vatican. Beneath the model houses and the Renaissance masterpiece, though, were the remains of the City's purgatorial cinder-and-ash landfill. A brochure that Robert Moses' Metropolitan Transit Authority self-published to advocate for the '64 fair evoked the area's pastoral history, albeit a version that expunged the first pre-colonial tenders of the land in a narrative that presaged the exclusionary legacy of Moses' impositions: "It was once a beautiful tidal basin, where farmers and townspeople harvested crops of salt hay, fish, crabs, clams, oysters and water fowl. … Then came Fishhooks McCarthy and his Brooklyn Ash Removal Company, and the once beautiful meadow became the gigantic ash dump of Scott Fitzgerald's 'Great Gatsby'." Borough rivalries aside—hard to imagine that only Brooklyn cinders filled the broad expanse—it was indeed

Fitzgerald who most lyrically described the intertwining in Queens of rural and industrial. Riding by on the train, his narrator was transfixed by what he saw: "This is a valley of ashes—a fantastic farm where ashes grow like wheat into ridges and hills and grotesque gardens…" From cinders to cinderblocks, contemporary Queens gardeners remain preternaturally capable of finding purpose in what others see as waste. The gardener's joy at patternmaking, shaping, and embellishment does not, at least in Queens, preclude the use of such discards as plastic storage bins, trash can lids, milk crates, and grocery store shopping baskets as components integral to the landscaping. Salvaged cinderblock, known nowadays as concrete block, serves as a stepped display pedestal for flower pots, including one embellished by a lime-green-leafed plastic garland. Lush plants share space with trash cans and recycling bins. The alchemy that for Fitzgerald's hero acted as a metaphor for the grotesque has taken on positive value in an era that has new-found admiration for old-school tinkerers and their genius for reuse.

Queens is statistically the New York City borough in which the most languages are spoken; it is also a borough of enormous biodiversity, home to some of the City's very few freshwater wetlands, just south of the park that Moses built above the cinder dump. It makes sense that Queens gardens are touchstones between far-flung places and native ecotones. In gardens, unlike streetscapes in which diasporic identity can be signaled by lettering on signs or figurative elements on façades, self-expression is achieved by calibrating the everyday and the particular. The plants at stake may in themselves be simple regulars from the landscape section of any big-box do-it-yourself store: hydrangeas, begonias, boxwood, juniper, impatiens, marigolds. But when combined according to the gardener's sensibilities, they take on qualities that their standard suburban counterparts only dream of. Or, inversely, everyday artifacts are used to scaffold plants whose morphologies standard garden centers covet. Ingenuity is needed to negotiate the straits of the urban garden in New York City and its climate, witness the image of a fig tree, wrapped for winter, protected from freezing rains and snow by a bucket slung over its crown. For the intrepid lover of fresh figs, there is no bad weather, as the saying goes, just the wrong jacket. And although the book opens with topiary, a skill as difficult to master as fine cabinetry or haircutting or tailoring or any of the other "measure twice, cut once" crafts, it quickly departs from a conventional definition of gardening as plant life dependent. Astroturf, paint, fences and railings, fountains, statuary: Queens gardens have found ways to outsmart the seasonal rhythms that preclude all-year-round tropical brights or geometric textural play.

On studying the images in each section and reading the carefully appreciative texts that accompany them, it's worth considering whether those who created and tend these gardens do so as an act of civic generosity or as a gesture of playful impudence towards the city in which they reside. Maybe it's both at once. To build a rock garden as complex as the Watts Towers, to position a silvered Buddha towards the public thoroughfare: these are unquestionably gestures of grace towards one's neighbors. They are also predicated on conviction, hard work, and belief. To drape an alleyway or sidewalk with an arbor of bitter melon, or to cover a paved-over front yard in a bright checkerboard of burnt sienna and egg-yolk yellow might easily be construed differently, however: a refusal to be confined by the dictates of private property or of grey, ugly winter. Here, too, the truth might be both/and. What better could a Queens garden be than a vibrant, joyous version of the core conflict of life in America, individual expression and dedication to the common good in one?

Sarah Kam, 'Long Island City Viewed through the Evolution of Bread.' [Unpublished research paper], December 15, 2017

NYC Department of Parks, 'The Alley Pond Giant.' https://www.nycgovparks.org/parks/alley-pond-park/highlights/19645 Accessed May 13, 2025

Rudolph Burckhardt and Edwin Denby, 'A Walk through Astoria and Other Places in Queens' (1943). Exhibition, Bruce Silverstein Gallery, September 14-November 21, 2017. https://brucesilverstein.com/exhibitions/37-a-walk-through-astoria-and-other-places-in-by-rudolph-burckhardt-edwin-denby/overview/ Accessed May 13, 2025

Robert Moses, 'The Saga of Flushing Meadows.' (Metropolitan Transit Authority: New York, 1966)

Rebecca Solnit and Joshua Jelly-Shapiro, Non-Stop Metropolis: A New York City Atlas. (University of California Press: Oakland, 2016)

Natural Areas Conservancy, 'NYC Nature Map.' https://naturalareasnyc.org/nyc-nature-map Accessed May 13, 2025

DITMARS-STEINWAY
LA GUARDIA AIRPORT
RAVENSWOOD
ASTORIA
ASTORIA HEIGHTS
EAST ELMHURST
QUEENSBRIDGE
JACKSON HEIGHTS
NORTH CORONA
WOODSIDE
LONG ISLAND CITY
SUNNYSIDE
CORONA
ELMHURST
LEFRAK CITY
MIDDLE VILLAGE
REGO PARK
MASPETH
FOREST HILLS
GLENDALE
FOREST PARK
RIDGEWOOD
WOODHAVEN
OZONE PARK
LINDENWOOD
HOWARD BEACH
SEA SIDE
ROCKAWAY PARK
BELLE HARBOR
NEPONSIT
ROXBURY
BREEZY POINT
NEW YORK CITY
BRONX
MANHATTAN
QUEENS
BROOKLYN
STATEN ISLAND

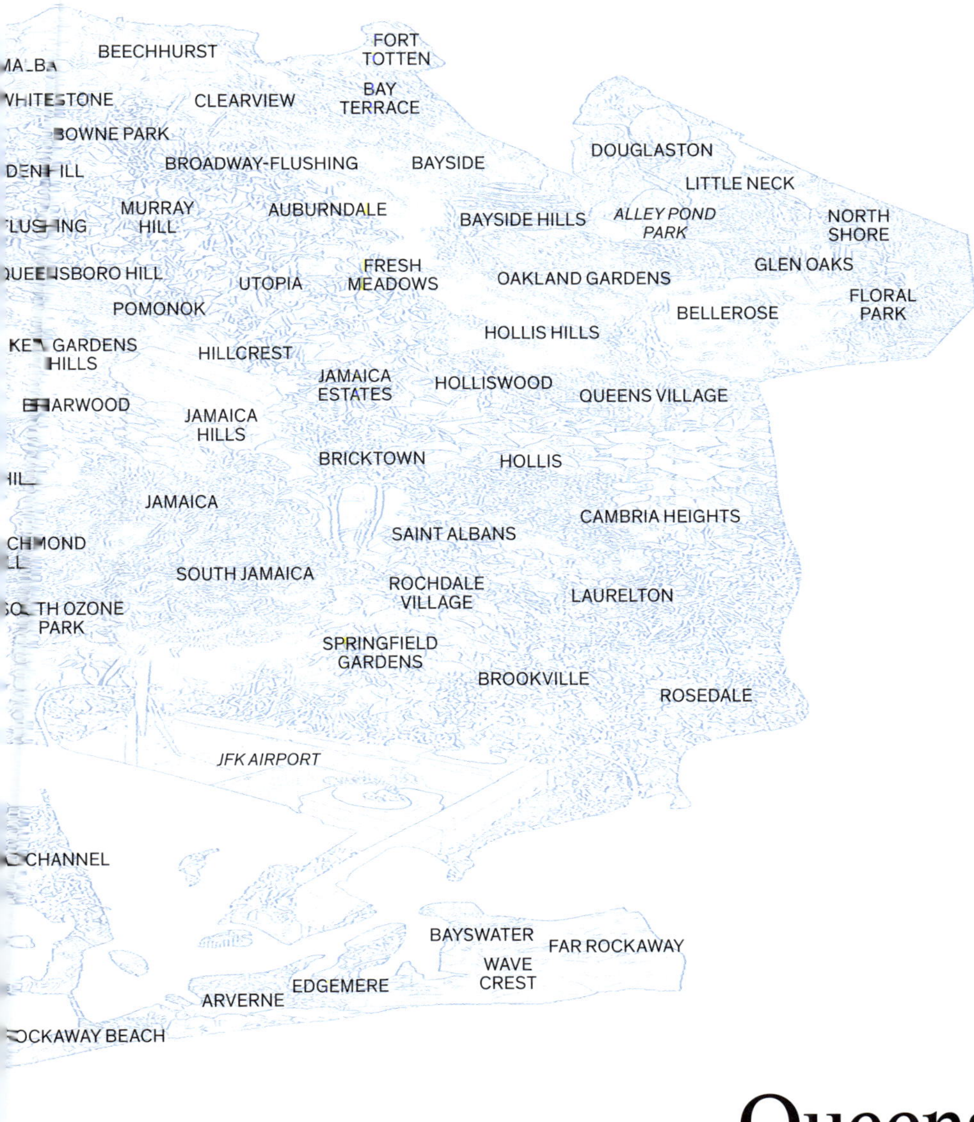

Queens Neighborhoods

Formal Gardens

AUBURNDALE
BAYSIDE
BELLEROSE
BOWNE PARK
BROADWAY-FLUSHING
CLEARVIEW
FOREST HILLS
HOLLISWOOD
HOWARD BEACH
JAMAICA ESTATES
KEW GARDENS HILLS
LAURELTON
MIDDLE VILLAGE
SOUTH OZONE PARK
SOUTH RICHMOND HILL
WHITESTONE

Front Yard Crescent

BAYSIDE | 2018

The crescent topiary formation on this small multi-family tract, with its Federalist stylings, is the real showstopper on the block. While the majority of the neighbors have maintained a clearly visible footpath leading straight to the front door with minimal landscaping, the garden of this front yard makes use of the already paved driveway for pedestrian access to gain another six feet of width (three feet each side). It also serves to screen the main entrance—a common strategy in Queens—with the shape of the English yew providing an increased sense of privacy as one approaches the front door.

Sidewalk Sushi Knots

KEW GARDENS HILLS | 2024

Within the winding, hilly streets of suburban Kew Gardens Hills, this striking front garden of stepped topiary knots is filled with impatiens and, at the back, a twiggy Japanese maple. The colorful, geometric design of these low-slung boxwoods brings to mind the premade sushi trays put on display at many New York City markets. This botanical version that is being offered to visitors and passersby comes right to the edge of the sidewalk, separated by a thin brick curb that matches the tone of the stone pavers of the sunken driveway on the right and the landing of the stepped entrance to the left.

Blue Atlas Cedar Archway

BROADWAY-FLUSHING | 2024

At this typical single-story suburban tract house in the northeastern section of the borough, two Blue Atlas cedars reach out over the sidewalk and create an archway over the steps leading to the front door. Similar to the garden on the previous page (*Sidewalk Sushi Knots*), the brick flower beds provide a structured layout to the front garden that cleanly separates the main entry from the driveway and the gentle ramp to the left. The different paths and level changes of the front garden are accentuated by thick white tubular rails, offering a strong counterpoint to the weeping organic shapes.

Millennial Gray Garden

SOUTH RICHMOND HILL | 2024

Vinyl cladding and painted brick are coordinated in a cool millennial gray color scheme to frame a single, almost spherical, English yew shrub in the front yard of this single-family home. “One tree” gardens are common throughout Queens as space is limited and this focuses all the attention on the botanical specimen. This example in the southwestern section of the borough might be the most extreme I’ve encountered, given that there is no other organic material, not even mulch. In this front garden the tree seems to grow right out of the pavement!

Green Boulder Bouncer

AUBURNDALE | 2024

At this semi-detached brick house in northeastern Queens, an unusually tall and boulder-shaped hedge with a flat top is situated like a bouncer in front of a club, guarding the front door and driveway. In lieu of the velvet rope, a carpet of red-and-white petunias serves as the well-mannered barrier. The pedestrian access to the house follows a branch-shaped path that bends around the large bush, while access to the rear yard continues in a straight line past the neighbor's white urn.

Corner Boulder

WHITESTONE | 2024

Another boulder-shaped hedge perched at the edge of a sidewalk garden surprises passerby on a quiet residential street in the northeastern section of Queens. In this case, the large topiary form is used to soften the corner of the neighbor's chest-high brick retaining wall that contains a white-pebbled garden, separating the driveways of two single-family houses on a hilly street. This "hanging" rock garden has a humorous urban Zen character that combines a couple of sculptural rocks with two errant basketballs and a rabbit lawn ornament that has fallen over.

Hanging Mochi Garden

HOLLISWOOD | 2024

Even more dramatic than the previous boulder-shaped topiary gardens, this raised garden with mochi-shaped topiary overhangs a retaining wall. The suburban "hanging garden" of sorts clusters most of the formal elements around the curving stair that leads to the front entrance of this ranch-style single-family home in southeastern Queens. The rest of the front yard is carpeted with synthetic grass and dotted with colorful impatiens along the edge above the sidewalk.

Mochi Still Life

MIDDLE VILLAGE | 2024

Another prominent "mochi-shaped" hedge foregrounds a collection of rounded topiary shapes comprised of cones and cylinders, resembling a still life arrangement. This long strip garden projects out to the edge of the sidewalk from the recessed street wall of a redbrick colonial row that is typical for Queens. The surprising pocket of formality contrasts with the other more unfinished front yard spaces on the block but also seems to elevate—and even incorporate—the neighbor's white lion finial and the pink petunia pot into the larger composition.

Front Yard Boxwood Parterre

HOWARD BEACH | 2024

One of the most formal gardens in Queens can be found at this Mediterranean-style Millennium mansion in Howard Beach. It features various boxwood parterres, whose radial patterns frame trees at the center (pp. 23–24) and crisscross lattice patterns that allow lampposts and flagpoles to pass through. This predominantly French tradition of gardening originated in royal palaces such as Versailles, where the preferred vantage point was from the second floor (*bel étage*). At this urban palace of sorts, a similar vantage point is provided by the many large windows and a balcony at the corner.

Stepped Scissor Hedges

KEW GARDENS HILLS | 2018

A more modest version of the previous boxwood designs graces the front yard of this suburban style home along the windy streets of Kew Gardens Hills. Adapting to the original slope of the site are three stepped terraces that contain hedges with an asymmetrical "scissor-style" pattern that favors the view from the street, not the second floor, placing this garden more in the Italian tradition of vertical gardens, as opposed to the flat carpet-like tradition found in the French countryside.

Donuts and Driveway Hors d'Oeuvres

LAURELTON | CLEARVIEW | 2023 | 2024

Some topiary gardens in Queens can almost make you hungry. At the above shrub-heavy example in Laurelton, a donut-shaped yew hedge—with yellow frosting—is coupled with a multi-tiered white birdbath that matches the other decorative objects (statues, urns, lampposts, etc.) that are sprinkled around this front garden like confections. To the right, a small round plate of "botanical hors d'oeuvres" floats in the middle of a suburban-style driveway in Clearview, offering up creeping juniper, boxwood, and yew, pinned together by a tall black toothpick in the shape of a lamppost.

Curbside Bar with Corkscrew Topiary

JAMAICA ESTATES | 2024

This curious conglomeration of topiary fronting the sidewalk is the last leg of a boxwood hedge that tracks around the front yard, marking the corners of the house and exterior stair with cones. Several associations come to mind, given its asymmetrical nature and various shapes, but the one I find most appealing is that of a baroque curbside bar with four squat stools—a piece of "virtual street furniture" for one of the most upscale neighborhoods in Queens that, even with its sidewalks, still feels very suburban.

Dr. Seuss Stair Garden

AUBURNDALE | 2019

Stair gardens are one of the interesting urban garden types in Queens, given that many of the single-family homes are in hilly neighborhoods and the stairs spill out onto the sidewalk. This example is so strange and fantastical that I named it after the bizarre children's book author, who was popular when I was a kid. It has a great collection of everyday topiary shapes (spirals, globes, and cones) and a pair of weeping Blue Atlas cedars. At the base of the stair, fulfilling the role of garden sentinels, are the ever-popular "hungry mochi" style topiaries, ready to bite any unwelcome guests.

Neo-Baroque Footpath

BAYSIDE | 2024

This single-family, split-level home with a two-car garage was pure Americana before a Queens landscaping company got hold of it. Now it embodies a "neo-baroque" spirit that conjures up images of lavish European gardens. In reality, it is just an elaborate footpath with an elliptical tree planter that winds out to the sidewalk between the driveway and the front lawn. Back at the house, two rounded tree planters help soften the corners and make the landscaping feel even more sculptural. These types of white marble step makeovers are quite common in Queens, but this is the boldest I've seen.

Home Is Where the Heart-Shaped Hedge Is

BELLEROSE | 2024

Here is another white marble footpath for a suburban home—this time in southeastern Queens—that is more two-dimensional in nature. It has a vase-like contour that bends around a heart-shaped tree and leads to the front door. This is one of the few examples of a Japanese maple being used for topiary in the borough, but it does follow the popular trend of “one tree” gardens, as discussed earlier (p. 17). The other botanical specimens: weeping cherry, weeping Norway spruce, blue spruce, yew, and arborvitae are all contained at the front of the house behind a curving stone planter wall.

Shaggy Maple

FOREST HILLS | 2024

An unruly Japanese maple in all its burgundy-colored glory is the highlight of this suburban-style garden with a big lawn and a few other low-slung bushes. Located at a prominent intersection in the northern part of Forest Hills, it is large enough to hide pedestrians who are about to turn the corner, especially those adolescents that attend the nearby high school. For them it is undoubtedly a natural landmark in the neighborhood, albeit seasonal.

Natty Juniper

SOUTH OZONE PARK | 2024

This highly expressive Hollywood juniper dominates the front yard of a single-family home in southwestern Queens. One barely sees past it to the house but can detect the light green color of the home's cladding that complements the vegetation. The main association I have with this type of tree in a tight enclosure is the walled cemeteries found throughout the Spanish countryside. In those cases, they are almost always tall and thin conical forms, the opposite of this “natty dread” branching expression.

Nymph Reunion

BOWNE PARK | 2024

This fantastical front garden on a suburban street in northeastern Queens is completely given over to topiary and statuary—no room left for humans! It features a crest-shaped Concorde Barberry hedge set into a maze-like pattern of boxwood, where four nymphs approach a concrete urn filled with pink petunias (see elevated view on pp. 36–37). This is one of my favorite botanical displays in the borough because of its tapestry-like design and the fact that it evokes the paintings of my Spanish uncle, Antonio Ferri, who often blends female figures into abstract Mediterranean landscapes.

Flower Gardens

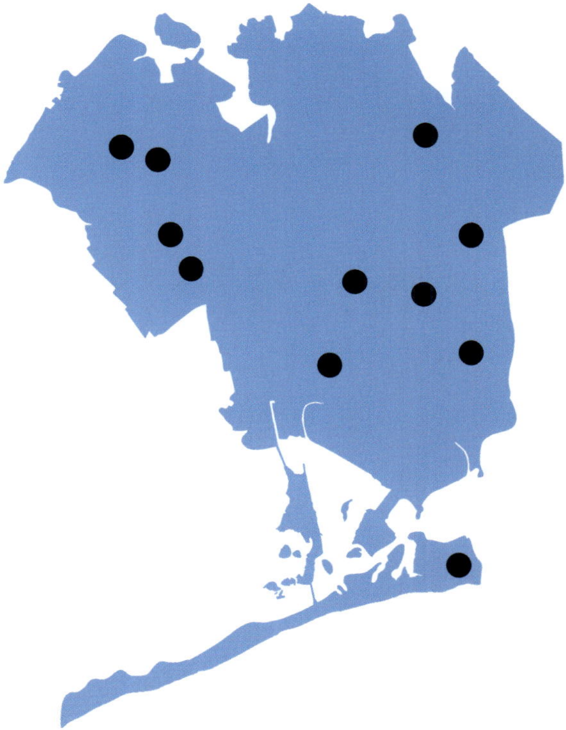

BAYSIDE
ELMHURST
FAR ROCKAWAY
GLENDALE
JAMAICA
LAURELTON
MIDDLE VILLAGE
QUEENS VILLAGE
SAINT ALBANS
SOUTH OZONE PARK
WOODSIDE

U.S. MAIL

Shalini's Flower Garden

SOUTH OZONE PARK | 2024

There are many brightly colored flower gardens in Queens, especially in the southern Indo-Caribbean neighborhoods, but none has packed in so many flower pots as the above homeowner in South Ozone Park. What is even more incredible to witness, especially within the context of New York City, is the sacrifice of an off-street parking space by the filling of the driveway with large flower pots—on stands, no less! In the wintertime, as Shalini's house is too small to bring in all the flowers, the local Hindu temple (*mandir*) picks up most, and her friends "plant-sit" the rest.

Lilac Cloud Parterre

SAINT ALBANS | 2018

This suburban tract house in southeastern Queens stands out for its unique lozenge-shaped parterre design filled with *Phlox douglasii* (aka Lilac Cloud). It takes advantage of the gentle slope of the front yard to tilt this floral carpet into view for all those who walk or drive by. A ribbon-shaped route provides access to the various planting beds from the front stair or driveway. The architecture of the home also contributes to the botanical spirit of this front garden through its ivy-patterned pressed-steel box columns.

Lilac Cloud Planter Bed

GLENDALE | 2018

A much smaller garden—also featuring *Phlox douglasii*—fronts this single-family home in Glendale. Backgrounded by pink evergreen azaleas, and the green asbestos siding of the porch, a pastel color scheme emerges. Many houses in this part of central Queens have opted for a more structured front yard design like the one above, employing planter beds in lieu of the original postage-stamp lawns (see right), which often require fencing to keep them clean as the neighborhood becomes more urban.

60 49

Sunken Drive Brights

MIDDLE VILLAGE | LAURELTON | 2023 | 2024

One of the most popular rowhouse types in Queens has a half flight of stairs up to the main living level and a half-level ramp down to the garage. Gardening along its narrow paths can be a challenge but one that homeowners willingly embrace. At the above house in southeastern Queens, a young gardener named Wazir has packed the walkway and porch with brightly colored annuals and a tropical banana plant that are meant to produce Florida vibes (his dream climate). To the left, a giant bouquet of chrysanthemums simply sits on the curb that separates the sunken drive from the walkway.

Josephine's Flower Garden

ELMHURST | 2024

Josephine is the family matriarch from Bangladesh responsible for this sprawling corner garden in central Queens. The random collection of flowers includes lilies, petunias, begonias, and delphiniums, among others. About half of the pots are protected from urban critters (i.e. rats and racoons) by loose welded wire grilles or galvanized metal mesh. This creates a strange dynamic between the natural and the industrial at a micro level that ends up defining the character of the garden. A few distinctive garden ornaments, like the young girl carrying a pot overhead, are also sprinkled into the mix.

Robinson's Window Garden

ELMHURST | 2023

Even more visceral than the previous entry is this window grille garden in the southern section of Elmhurst that spills out onto the sidewalk. (Some have remarked that the effect is more akin to vomiting.) Squash vines, evergreen shrubs, taro, perilla, and hot pink petunias are all clumped together in this small planting bed beside the front door. If we consider the history and theory of gardening for a minute, the person responsible for this rambunctious botanical display would probably align themselves with the sublime-loving Victorians or the cantankerous William Robinson, author of *The Wild Garden* (pub. 1870).

Annual Flowers and Red Brick Garden Walls

BAYSIDE | MIDDLE VILLAGE | 2024 | 2018

Red brick is one of the most common building materials in Queens. It is used for the exterior walls of houses and garden features alike. At the above rowhouse it contains a garden filled with impatiens, shrubs, and small lawn ornaments. On top of the porch railing wall is a bit of Queens surrealism, in the de Chirico tradition: a floating classical head planter with a dried-out dracaena is placed dead center, in line with the awning support. To the left is a red brick fence detail from Bayside where impatiens hang on either side of a single white baluster and geraniums bloom from the urn post cap above.

Angel Wing Begonias with Urns

LAURELTON | 2024

At these brick Tudor rowhouses in southeastern Queens, a grassy berm spans from the sidewalk to the deep setback of the front door. Contrasting with the rhythmic nature of the architecture that stretches down the block, this gardener captures our attention with a classical U-shaped scheme of angel wing begonias comprised of the shared hedge on the right, a series of urns sitting on the wide walkway to the left, and a short stretch in between at the front of the house.

Turtle Garden

WOODSIDE | 2023

This turtle carrying more than a dozen begonias on its back seems to be slowly making its way across a bed of sedum in a front garden packed with an eclectic mix of plant species. Towards the back is a shady spot under a climbing rose that contains a birdbath, a bench, and a Japanese stone lantern, but the rest of the garden is pretty much inaccessible, except for a few stepping stones and patches of dirt. A quiet garden on a not-so-quiet street just steps away from the Brooklyn-Queens Expressway.

Marigold Garden

QUEENS VILLAGE | 2018

Here is another U-shaped garden in southeastern Queens featuring flower beds of marigolds—similar to the red begonias from Laurelton on the previous spread—surrounding a small patch of grass. The color theme blends with the religious one towards the front door where *jhandi* flags (instruments of Hindu prayer typical of the Indo-Caribbean community in Queens) are planted on the side of the steps and marigold garlands are hung on the door grille. Paired with these religious symbols is the United States flag, adding an element of patriotism into this typical Queens multicultural mix.

Tree Trunk Hydrangeas

JAMAICA | 2024

If this were just a hydrangea bush in the middle of the front yard of a tract house, I probably would not have included it in a book about Queens gardens. But the creative repurposing of a dead tree trunk as a copper pot plant stand and a Japanese stone lantern podium with a blooming hydrangea bush at its base puts this squarely in the category of idiosyncratic urban gardening concepts that by and large define the private green spaces of the "World's Borough."

Jamaican Drive Court

FAR ROCKAWAY | 2024

This driveway garden in Far Rockaway—first seen on my house survey—was one of the main inspirations for this book about the private gardens of Queens. By creating a tropical-style forecourt to this modest mid-century multi-family development, it seems to be an even stronger manifestation of the borough's multicultural spirit than the shapes, materials, and bright colors that define its vernacular architecture. And to drive the point home even further, two Jamaican flags flank Old Glory on top of the mansard-style roof, as if this were a national pavilion of sorts (see following spread).

Mixed Pots and Plastic Containers

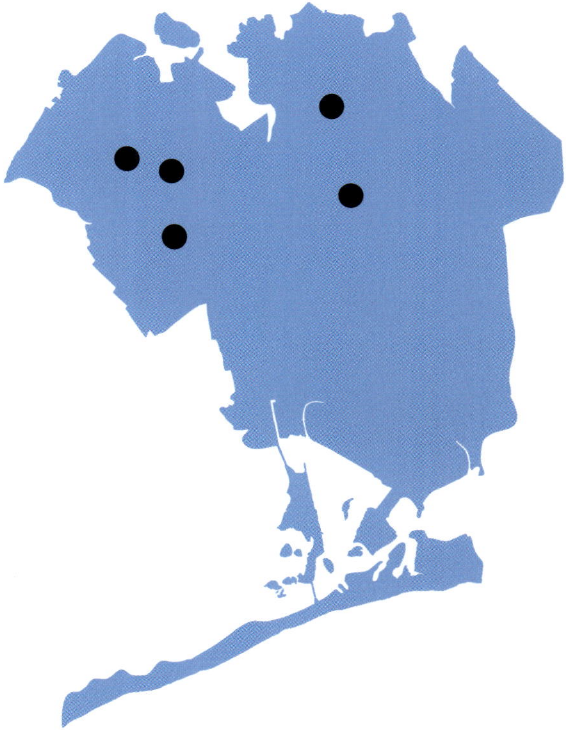

ELMHURST
HILLCREST
MIDDLE VILLAGE
MURRAY HILL
WOODSIDE

Side Yard Assemblage

ELMHURST | 2024

The garden element is all pervasive in Queens, even when there is seemingly no space to fit it in, like in the side yard of this corner house in Elmhurst. Here, amongst the hoses, brooms, rakes, and shovels—and several types of rainwater harvesting tanks—is a collection of twelve potted plants sitting on top of a discarded storm window that overhangs a caged IBC tote tank. The large plastic container is painted the same blue as the vinyl siding, in an attempt to blend it in and keep the focus on the plants above.

Moss Pole Still Life

ELMHURST | 2024

Here is another improvised garden at the base of a sunken driveway, mixing with the trash and recycling. The image of potted plants next to plastic bins implies that they are part of the trash (see also p. 62), but the deliberate placement of these plants with tall moss poles—spread out in an attempt to screen the bins—and the fact that they are in good health—makes it seem as if the intention here is to create a mini tropical garden next to the basement entrance of a typical mid-century Queens rowhouse.

Trash-and-Recycling Tableau

WOODSIDE | 2023

At this front yard, the order of pots and bins is reversed: trash, recycling, and compost in front, plants in back (bathing suits above). When I first walked by this informal arrangement, I thought these plants had been placed next to the refuse bins because they were being discarded, but when I looked more carefully, my impression was that of a colorful tableau of everyday objects that reduced the visual impact of these mandatory city containers—a bit of the "if you can't beat them, join them" mindset.

Storage Bin Sidewalk Garden

ELMHURST | 2023

This front yard is around the corner from the main intersection of Elmhurst, where the old Bank of the Manhattan Company building stands (presently occupied by Cathay Bank). It features four large plastic storage bins filled with bamboo and large pink hydrangeas pushed up to the line of the metal sidewalk grates that provide access to the building's utilities. Behind the bins is a small patch of English ivy and the trash-and-recycling station for this mid-size multi-family walk-up.

Sunken Cinder Block Garden

ELMHURST | 2023

On the site of a former filling station in central Queens, this sunken garden occupies the space left by underground petroleum tanks. A series of stepped cinder block supports with wood planks creates a bleacher-style arrangement of potted plants that this New York Botanical Garden employee enjoys experimenting with on the weekends. Jeffrey began his botanical project, like so many other young gardeners, during the dark days of Covid—just a few blocks from the US epicenter: Elmhurst Hospital. Sirens used to wail in the background. Today, thanks to his small urban oasis, birds come to sing.

Feng's Vegetable and Flower Garden

MURRAY HILL | 2024

Most Chinese gardens in Queens are exclusively dedicated to vegetables, but Feng's in Murray Hill has created a compelling "split garden" of sorts, with a bitter gourd pergola above and various flower pots and planting beds below. The result is a multi-colored carpet of petunias, marigolds, impatiens, and mums that is echoed at the rear of the garden in the form of a pastel-colored play mat footpath. This irrepressible spirit of recycling can be found throughout the garden and even in its irrigation strategy, which diverts roof water into two official NYC Environmental Protection rain barrels.

STOP

Post-War Balcony with Tropical Pots

MURRAY HILL | 2024

A couple of blocks away from the center of Koreatown, Queens (the Murray Hill stop on the Long Island Rail Road), this typical post-war walk-up has a full-width balcony, step-down awning, black iron picket fence, white S-scroll flat trusses, and over fifty houseplants of all shapes and sizes. Begonias, succulents, coleus, and a whole host of tropical species are planted in a variety of pots ranging from large, glazed ceramics to the original plastic liner from the store, and supported on all kinds of stands including unused furniture items, plastic storage shelving from Home Depot, and railing hooks.

Winter Fig Totem

HILLCREST | 2023

Fig tree protection has a long and, at times, comical tradition in New York City. This popular fruit tree from the Mediterranean and Southern Asia is grown in many immigrant communities throughout Queens and the other "outer boroughs." When winter arrives, strange assemblages wrap around them, involving cardboard boxes, plastic sheeting, foam boards, etc. But this Christo-like moment in Hillcrest, with its black walk-off mat and blue tarp, and an upside-down recycling bin that resembles an abstract contemporary sculpture, takes the cake. Kudos to Anthony in Hillcrest!

Milk Crate Garden Pedestals

ELMHURST | 2023

The side yard of this multi-family yellow brick building is in a remote corner of Elmhurst, tucked between the Long Island Expressway and the Jamaica-bound Long Island Rail Road. Normally, it looks like an informal patio with a mix of cheap outdoor furniture and potted plants strewn about in a random fashion. But the day I happened to walk past it in 2023, it was giving out subtle “garden vibes,” just from the fact that the pots were set on top of matching milk crate “pedestals” and equally spaced with the cobbled-together wood table to the left.

Brick Wall Gardens

ELMHURST | MIDDLE VILLAGE | 2024 | 2023

Another urban gardening trend that is popular in Queens is to line up potted plants of various types on top of brick walls. In the example above, the pots on the wall are mostly empty because a small roof has been built above, where the plants now grow. What's left below is more like a still life of random objects that combine with the ubiquitous blue rainwater collection barrel. On the following spread, a stepped planter wall is topped by a mix of blue and green ceramic pots—with a few terra cotta ones— displayed as if they were on the shelves of a home decorating store, not at the edge of a driveway!

Astroturf

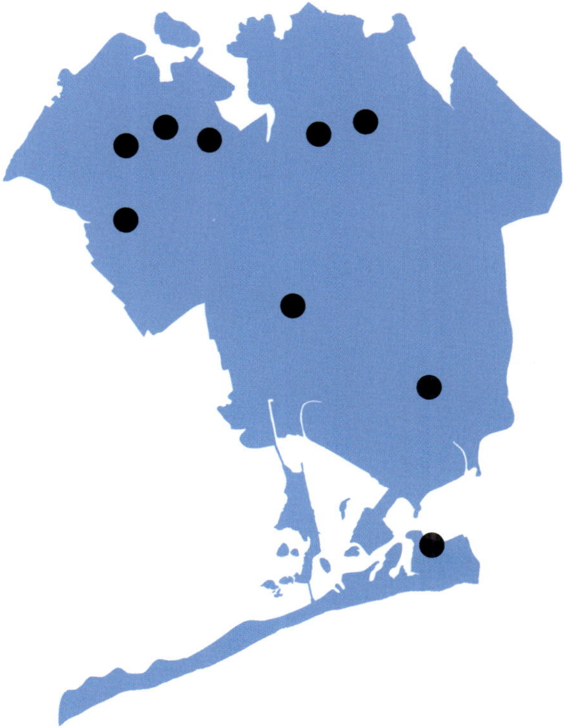

AUBURNDALE
BAYSWATER
CORONA
FLUSHING
JACKSON HEIGHTS
MASPETH
SOUTH RICHMOND HILL
SPRINGFIELD GARDENS
WOODSIDE

Green Party

WOODSIDE | 2024

Hung on the balcony railing of a small post-war apartment building like a political banner, this large sheet of synthetic grass seems to be missing a slogan. “Green Party” would be too ironic given the toxic nature of the material, but perhaps the most honest if this were to represent the pre-urban, pastoral landscape filled with farms and golf courses that many Queens residents long for. A lot to read into an ad-hoc privacy panel, I realize, but perhaps a little of what is bubbling under the surface.

Yellow Astro/Green Turf

SPRINGFIELD GARDENS | 2024

In this front yard in southeastern Queens we have a literal representation of Astroturf with an artificial green grass lawn and a yellow star inlay. It's probably not a homage to the Houston Astros—the baseball team responsible for popularizing the synthetic grass material—since the star has eight points and not five like their logo, but it "brands" this single-family home's private green space with a memorable motif that stands out in the neighborhood.

Diamond Grid with Green Ivy

SOUTH RICHMOND HILL | 2024

The front garden of this typical mock-Tudor developer house in southwestern Queens used to contain a small tree, hedgerows, and a paved footpath. The new design boasts a diagonal grid pattern highlighted with Astroturf strips between the concrete pavers and plastic ivy wrapped around the columns of the covered entrance. The absence of any patio furniture or botanical theme—save the three pots at the back—speaks to the front yard's new formal character, a formality that is somewhat undermined by the ubiquitous orange parking cone, a mainstay of the Queens front garden in the more urban neighborhoods.

AstroPorch

CORONA | 2023

Here is another elevated planting bed that has evolved into a more artificial, urban garden. Just a block from the 7 Train and around the corner from a mobile fruit vendor, this covered outdoor space seems to merely evoke the notion of a green space without actually using it for anything (note the absence of patio furniture, plants, etc.). Perhaps this is because of its proximity to a subway stop, or the fact that the newly renovated stair bypasses the planter bed level without providing a landing.

Turf Carpet and Granite Porch

FLUSHING | 2024

In the above front yard in East Flushing is a typical lawn replacement using Astroturf. The effect is really closer to an exterior green carpet that is simply meant to soften the patio hardscape and create a buffer between the dining patio and the main entrance, leaving a skinny path of brick and precast pavers connecting the two. Looking over this turf feature—and interlocking with it visually—is a brick porch filled with gray granite balusters and Corinthian-style fluted columns.

Putting Green Parking Strips

AUBURNDALE | 2018

At this curious multi-family building with "silo" stair enclosures, the original strips of grass separating the driveways are gradually being replaced with Astroturf. They conjure up images of putting greens or mini-golf holes that harken back to a time when the borough was filled with golf courses. At the middle strip, a garden idea might be beginning to happen where three empty terra cotta pots flank the turf. But for now, these flat green strips of synthetic grass are more like suburban-style parterres—plain green exterior "rugs," rolled out to the curb.

36 18

Outdoor Living

MASPETH | BAYSWATER | JACKSON HEIGHTS | 2023 | 2024 | 2022

In contrast with the previous examples of Astroturf, which featured mostly traditional applications of the material as replacement grass or decorative accents, these last three gardens showcase outdoor spaces used for living, dining, and recreation. On the driveway above, patio furniture is arranged atop synthetic grass rugs, making the front of the house look more like the back. To the right, an outdoor barbecue area is enveloped in synthetic grass sheets that even tuck into the rear corner of the house. The following spread shows a fully turfed "play villa" with potted arborvitae on the balcony.

92 02

Fountains

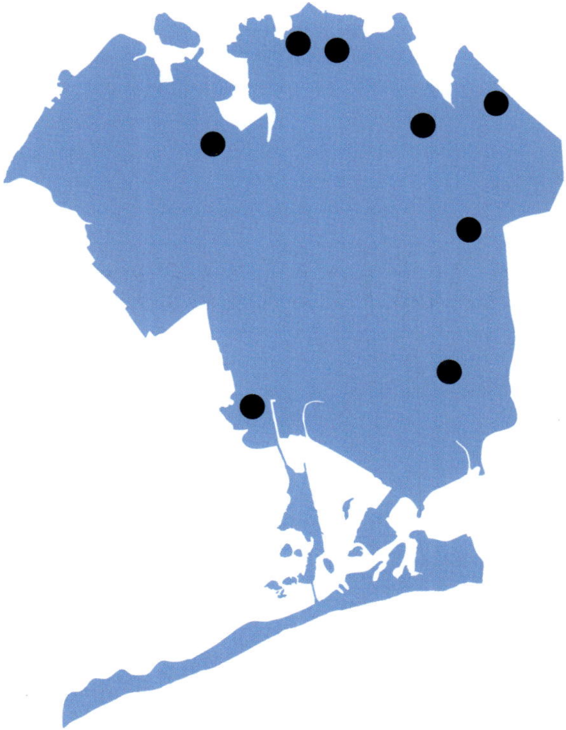

BAYSIDE
CORONA
HOWARD BEACH
LAURELTON
LITTLE NECK
MALBA
QUEENS VILLAGE
WHITESTONE

93 FOUNTAINS

Suburban Apparitions

QUEENS VILLAGE | BAYSIDE | 2024

At the small Mediterranean-style stucco house above, in a suburban neighborhood of northeastern Queens, the typical front yard lawn has slowly given way to a small waterfall scene set within tapered topiary shrubs and trimmed with a crescent-shaped flower bed filled with impatiens and begonias. Not as surreal as the Blue Atlas cedar "phantom" and twisting faux rock fountain to the left, but something of a portal into one's imagination, especially mine—having spent much of my childhood exploring the gorges of the Finger Lakes region of Western New York State.

Shan Shui Fountain

LITTLE NECK | 2024

Foregrounding this small millennial mansion in a neighborhood bordering Nassau County (Long Island) is this Chinese rock fountain emerging out of a stone base with a crisp circula opening a little larger than the size of a manhole. Morning glory vine and trailing succulents have started to grow on top, and moss is appearing on its shady ledges. The irregular forma quality that pays homage to nature and the *shan shui* theme of "mountain" and "water"—present in many of the most important Chinese gardens and landscape paintings—is the centerpiece of this garden.

Clamshell Laundry Maiden

LAURELTON | 2018

At the opposite end of Queens from the previous garden—where the Chinese population is practically non-existent—this colorful fountain foregrounds a modest semi-detached house. This fountain, in a decidedly western tradition, combines the popular clamshell motif with a young maiden on top. The design recalls iconic works of Italian art such as Botticelli's *Birth of Venus*, but, upon closer inspection, one sees that this is a depiction not of idealized beauty but of the everyday chore of doing laundry—a domestic theme very much at home in working-class Queens.

Blue Stork Fountain

HOWARD BEACH | 2024

At the above suburban house in Howard Beach, another mini-waterfall front garden occupies the slice of green space between the driveway and a curved footpath leading to the main entrance at the side of the structure. It contains an eclectic mix of plant species including the popular weeping Blue Atlas cedar, creeping juniper, hosta, English ivy, variegated lilyturf, and a large Alaska cedar at the rear. But the star of this garden scene is really the metallic blue stork at the foot of the falls (facing page) that acts as a friendly gatekeeper and conjures up a sense of fantasy at the same time.

Koi Ponds

HOWARD BEACH | CORONA | LITTLE NECK | 2024

Koi ponds are quite popular in Queens. The above example is bordered by yellow sedum in the foreground and "protected" by an English bulldog ornament. To the right, the koi pond is "protected" by a divine force: the Virgin Mary. Her precast niche sits pond-side next to the shady "grotto-like" spot created by a Japanese maple, and the koi gather round. The following spread shows a koi "superhighway" in Little Neck that connects two ponds at opposite ends of a backyard. It is protected by bent metal grilles, recalling the gritty pedestrian overpasses of the Long Island Expressway.

Side Yard Rockery

MALBA | 2024

Up until this point, the fountains imitating waterfalls featured in this book have been miniaturized versions of what one would encounter in nature. This Chinese rock garden in the northeastern neighborhood of Malba is the exception, in that it is almost life-size. Malba, the wealthiest neighborhood in Queens, is filled with large, ostentatious single-family homes (i.e. millennial mansions), but at this modest mid-century residence, it is the garden that has all the drama, especially towards the street, where the fountain cascades down to a pool five feet above the sidewalk (facing page and overleaf).

Rear Patio Rock Garden

LITTLE NECK | 2024

Here is another rockery-style garden by a Chinese homeowner in northeastern Queens that is still "under construction" on the rear patio of a large single-family home in Little Neck. The design is focused on a medium-sized waterfall at the corner of the property that spills into a blue mosaic pool. Miniature temples and other cast resin ornaments are strewn about, including a couple of floating ducks. In the foreground is a collection of large rocks that have yet to find their way into this kitschy garden composition. But for the time being, they slightly evoke images of the poetic "scholar's gardens" of Ancient China.

Suburban Seduction

BAYSIDE | 2024

Probably the most erotic front lawn scene in all of Queens—although the next garden could also be a contender—the above fountain featuring a siren being hoisted up by an adoring male figure who is holding her fish-scaled buttocks is a real showstopper. On the corner of a typical suburban street in the northeastern section of the borough, the two glistening bronze-plated bodies cavort in the middle of an octagonal pool, presenting a striking counterpoint to the image of conservative "family values" usually associated with these types of American communities.

Salvatore's Sea Shell Extravaganza

WHITESTONE | 2024

Since the year 2000, Salvatore of Palermo has been transforming his front yard into a monumental work of folk art consisting of two lobe-shaped water features. These flank the front entrance of his modest home on a quiet street in Whitestone. Dominating the left planter is a phallic-shaped fountain with a mule in front. The right planter consists of a castle-like structure with a river running behind it that ends in a green water basin (see following spread). The sea shells that cover these fantastical garden motifs were collected from Long Beach, just across the Queens border in Nassau County.

Chinese Vegetable Gardens

CORONA
ELMHURST
FLUSHING
MASPETH
QUEENSBORO HILL
WOODSIDE

Sidewalk Vegetable Pergola

QUEENSBORO HILL | 2023

On a slowly gentrifying residential street in Greater Flushing, this Chinese urban farmer has fashioned a small vegetable garden that juts out towards the sidewalk between the sloping driveways of a tract of attached housing typical for Queens. It grows from a narrow planting bed on the right, containing sweet potato plants and buried buckets of tomato vines, and spans over the concrete footpath on an improvised pergola. Long squash dangle overhead as you approach the front steps and brightly colored plastic growing bins line the edge of the driveway to the left, warning of the level change.

Back Alley Garden Plots

MASPETH | 2023

Behind the brick rowhouses of Queens one often finds a series of small plots corresponding to the width of each property. These spaces are not usually deep enough for a parking stall but are the perfect size for Chinese vegetable gardens. The one above sits on a level concrete plinth and is fully covered with bottle gourd and bean vines. Beneath the thick canopy, a garden shed is cobbled together with scraps of lumber and half a dozen five-gallon buckets filled with lemongrass. On its left (facing page) is a more accessible plot with mix-matched "disco" pavers below a winter melon pergola.

Long Squash Garden Patio

FLUSHING | 2024

This is the most "engineered" vegetable pergola I've come across in Queens. (At first glance, I confused it with a carport.) The low-profile trusses span the entire rear patio to create a column-free space filled with very long squashes. These dangle down at head height making it a challenge to walk around freely on the patio. Connecting to the front yard of the house is another elegant garden structure—for Queens standards—made of half-round hoops that allow for a barrel-shaped greenhouse when covered with plastic sheeting in the colder months (facing page).

Green Hazard Garden

ELMHURST | 2023

Compared with the previous garden, this is probably the least "engineered" trellis in all of Queens—and the most expeditious. Green plastic hazard netting is simply draped, like laundered sheets, over wires that run between the steel corner posts. It creates this dense canopy of chayotes, some resting on top, others dangling beneath, making one feel as if one is almost underwater. It seems contradictory that plastic and nature could coexist in this manner, but at least in the short term—before the UV rays do their damage—there is an uncanny type of symbiosis at work.

Orange Hazard Garden

QUEENSBORO HILL | 2023

Here is another informal front garden that makes use of hazard netting and doesn't even need to string up wire or erect steel posts. Taking advantage of the existing level change between the raised patio and the sidewalk planting bed, a pitched hammock-like canopy has been tied to their respective stainless steel railings, allowing for head height access on the south side of the garden. Hanging directly over the cored brick path that cuts across the garden, a ten-pound winter melon in a smaller hammock-like sling has been affixed to the open grid of the orange hazard netting.

Big Bottle Jockstraps

MASPETH | 2023

Throughout history, humorous associations have been made between the gourd family (aka Cucurbitaceae) and human anatomy. To cite one example, the fantastical Italian Renaissance painter Giuseppe Arcimboldo used many of its species to define the facial features of his subjects. But in the Chinese vegetable gardens of Queens the humor goes beyond the bulbous—often suggestive—shapes of the various species to include their improvised support systems. The above example fashions jockstrap-style slings for several big bottle gourds out of orange fishnet fabric.

Winter Melon Shoplifting

ELMHURST | 2023

The image of an abandoned shopping cart by the side of the road is often used as a negative symbol of American consumerism and neglect. By contrast, in New York City it is common to see broken-down shopping carts repurposed by street food vendors selling everything from flavored ice *raspadillas* to fried empanadas. In the Chinese vegetable garden above, far removed from street vendors or any other commercial activity, we see a rare upcycling of bright red store-branded shopping baskets into winter melon scaffolding—an image of consumerism undercut by "DIY-ism."

Rowhouse Garden Rows

QUEENSBORO HILL | 2023

Various forms of urban farming fill up the front setback of these typical brick rowhouses in the southern section of Queensboro Hill. On the sunken driveway (above), calibrated to parked car dimensions, is a variety of leafy potted vegetables and pepper plants. To the left, a Styrofoam "barge" of Chinese cabbage covered with green netting and large white bins with edible chrysanthemums. To the right, a bright red Amaranthus that matches the step-down awnings of the front porches. And on the following spread, the view from the side illustrates the effect of urban "garden rows" on this block.

White Lattice/Spiderweb Trellis

CORONA | 2024

Wedged between a large brick Fedders building and a busy avenue in the heart of Corona is a small farm plot like the kind you would normally see on the outskirts of a modern city! It is divided into two sections: one with a shed and garden rows bordered by white lattice, the other covered by a kabocha squash vine trellis. The latter is cobbled together using clotheslines, wire, and scraps of lumber attached to the tips of the converging steel fences like a built version of cat's cradle. Below this, a typical assortment of loose pots, plastic bins, and an old tire painted to look like terra cotta.

Plastic Bucket Gardens

WOODSIDE | MASPETH | 2023

Repurposed plastic buckets are the mainstay of Chinese vegetable gardens in Queens. After the paint job is complete or the cat litter has been used, they make their way to the garden as oversized pots. The most common types are the round, five-gallon, yellow and white variety (orange ones from Home Depot are also very popular), or the four-gallon square variety, almost always in yellow. On the right, bucket totems are strapped together with an NYC brown composting bin and upside-down flower pot in an attempt to support two enormous winter melons that hang from a flimsy improvised pergola.

KEEP REFRIGERATED AT
RESTAURANT

Blue Plastic Wonderland

MASPETH | 2023 | 2024

The other colorful pieces of plastic found in almost all Queens Chinese vegetable gardens are the 55-gallon blue rain barrels. They are usually clustered near a downspout in order to easily redirect the water. In the above driveway garden, the homeowner has spliced in four rubber hoses. On the other side of the driveway—under the zucchini carport—the barrels are cut in half to produce two open container planters filled with A-Choy lettuce. In the patio garden to the left, a blue plastic kiddie pool, with about half the capacity of the rain barrel (20 gal), is filled with water spinach.

NYC
FOOD
&
YARD
WASTE

Garden Walls and Iron Fences

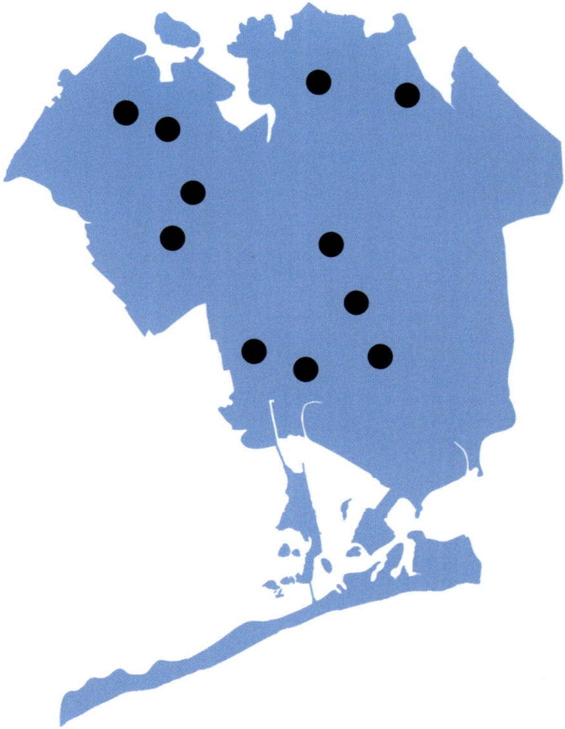

BAYSIDE
BOWNE PARK
BRIARWOOD
JACKSON HEIGHTS
JAMAICA
MIDDLE VILLAGE
OZONE PARK
REGO PARK
SOUTH JAMAICA
SOUTH OZONE PARK
WOODSIDE

Blue Rail Roundup

WOODSIDE | 2024

Freshly painted blue railings, although low in height, provide a strong visual barrier to this chaotic mix of boxwood, rose bushes, hydrangeas, and the popular weeping Blue Atlas cedar that is planted in front of this post-war multi-family walk-up with artificial ivy privacy screens on the balcony railings. Perhaps the bright color is creeping over from the Greek part of Astoria, where countless railings and pergolas are painted in a similar fashion. In the side garden (overleaf), a more peaceful approach—despite the cultivar's name—employs a single Thundercloud Plum tree bordered by a golden Euonymus.

Sunflower Sidewalk Garden

BRIARWOOD | 2018

Parked out in front of this house in southeastern Queens is a small sidewalk garden that feels like a botanical crib of sorts. It connects visually to the main garden fence since this also has some painted color, but ends up attracting all the attention away from it thanks to its more elaborate folksy design of yellow sunflowers and multi-colored cattails. The homeowners do not seem the least bit protective about their "child" but instead offer it to the neighborhood as a public mini-garden of sorts—like the kind one stumbles across at small traffic islands throughout the city.

Faux Branchwork Balustrade

BAYSIDE | 2024

This unusual balustrade with a faux branchwork pattern encloses a large patio in front of a medium-size brick house in the northeastern neighborhood of Bayside. Traditionally, garden enclosures do not mimic natural forms so literally (the previous garden, *Sunflower Sidewalk Garden*, is another exception to this rule), but in this case, where the front yard is mostly a hardscaped extension of the living quarters, it perhaps makes more sense to attempt to create a garden environment from the inside looking out than from the outside looking in.

Scalloped Breezeblock

JACKSON HEIGHTS | 2018

This is one of the more interesting urban garden enclosures I have come across in my many surveys of Queens. Located in the eastern section of Jackson Heights, just a couple of blocks away from the North Corona border, it uses standard breezeblock for the base of the fence but scallops the top to allow for a view of the front garden patio floor that is filled with flower pots and an arborvitae. It is painted red and white to coordinate with the entry porch awning and security is maintained by black ironwork consisting of straight pickets and S-scrolls topped with spear tip fence posts.

Muhammed's Wave Wall

SOUTH JAMAICA | 2024

This is how bricklayers freestyle. Without any drawings, Muhammed envisioned a brick wave around his house and got busy laying bricks. Months later he had this striking garden wall with alternating colors, changing orientations, and a sinuous top. Behind the wavy profile is a planter bed filled with corn stalks. It is somewhat surprising to see this crop along an urban sidewalk but it is part of the larger "kitchen garden" program of the home and functions quite well as a screen to the elevated patio behind, which would otherwise be exposed to a busy corner in southeastern Queens.

Steel Wheels

MIDDLE VILLAGE | 2023

Here is another scalloped garden enclosure that has one of the most peculiar combinations of solid wall and steel fencing in the borough, which is made even stranger by its orange-and-black Halloween color scheme. Wrought-iron wheels with spear-tip spokes are clipped into each of the semi-circular scallops that are shaped of brick and covered with stucco. Currently, there is not much garden behind this garden wall, but the potential exists for something spectacular should the "steel wheel" design be exploited. Perhaps a maritime theme with a water feature?

Leak Fence

BOWNE PARK | 2024

This concrete fence provides an intriguing screened view of the front yard of a contemporary two-family home in northeastern Queens. It recalls the intricate lattice designs employed for windows in classical Chinese gardens (*lou chuang*, aka "leak windows"), as well as the weathered gray stone typically used for railings and walls. Hopefully, this is the first step towards a more poetic makeover that will layer more culture and meaning onto this front garden space.

Lord Hanuman Porch Garden

OZONE PARK | 2024

Two levels of wide-set balusters reveal a series of potted flowers and plants in this brightly colored porch garden. Hanging from the aluminum awning are petunias and a Boston fern. On the porch and patio, more petunias and hibiscus. To the left, a large “bouquet” of *jhandi* flags, the Hindu prayer flags popular with the Indo-Caribbean population of Queens. Also popular in this section of the borough are monochromatic color schemes that express devotion to a single deity. In this case, the homeowner is paying tribute to Lord Hanuman, the monkey god, whose favorite color is red.

Diamond Patterns and Diapering

REGO PARK | SOUTH OZONE PARK | JAMAICA | 2024

Queens, for the most part, is averse to blank surfaces. The practice of using diagonal patterns to produce diamond shapes in architecture is called diapering and is alive and well in the "World's Borough." One can find many variations of these on garden walls, especially in more urban situations, where there is a need for some privacy and protection from the sidewalk. The examples included here are found on a blue-and-white garden wall in South Ozone Park (above), a chain-link fence with privacy slats in Rego Park (left), and a pink garden wall in Jamaica with glaring cat eyes (overleaf).

Q42

Painted Gardens and Sidewalk Parterres

HOLLIS
MASPETH
MIDDLE VILLAGE
QUEENS VILLAGE
RICHMOND HILL
SAINT ALBANS
SOUTH JAMAICA
SOUTH OZONE PARK
SOUTH RICHMOND HILL

Pink-Walled Paradise

RICHMOND HILL | 2024

This is the first house on a busy mixed-use boulevard in Richmond Hill that transitions the block from commercial to residential. It does so boldly with a bright pink perimeter wall—with maroon and indigo accents—that pushes past the 99 cent store to the right and renders the neighbor's chain-link fence almost invisible. This "pink-walled paradise" evokes the origin story of gardens as idealized botanical spaces set apart from the wilderness and chaos of the world and applies it to the "concrete jungle" context that is slowly overtaking this section of southwestern Queens.

Aqua Porch with Gravel Beds

SOUTH RICHMOND HILL | 2024

This white gravel bed edged with red rock presents a “blank canvas” image of a rock garden framed with bright aqua sleeper boards. On the next gravel bed—another two sleeper boards high—three flowering shrubs struggle to surpass the porch level. And at this uppermost level is the seating area with four white plastic chairs for accommodating guests and staying connected to the street life of this southwestern Queens neighborhood. The aqua color scheme continues on the stucco wall of the porch, ensuring that this protruding volume of the house is also part of the garden.

Four-Panel Pea Gravel Garden

QUEENS VILLAGE | 2024

Who says your front yard ends at the sidewalk? Many Queens homeowners continue their garden themes on the other side and let the sidewalk pass right on through. This pea gravel garden in southeastern Queens appears to be almost twice the size of the neighbors' front yards—and to have more impact as well—by cleverly matching the pea gravel beds on both sides of the sidewalk and continuing the footpath out to the curb. It is interesting to note that, in order to keep the focus on these four parterre "panels," the pavers around the steps are of a red brick color that blends with the house.

Sidewalk Sled

SOUTH RICHMOND HILL | 2024

Here is another bold front garden design that is not afraid to engage the sidewalk. This "sidewalk sled" filled with sedum, hostas, hydrangeas, and an English yew slides down from the raised planter bed to a minimal curb height at the property line—or perhaps a few feet over? The curvilinear retaining wall is painted light yellow to match the risers of the stair and to connect it to the stoop architecture of this single-family home in southwestern Queens. To the right, above the garage, the garden program continues with a dark green artificial ivy fence wrapping around a raised terrace.

Stone-and-Rubber Parterre

MIDDLE VILLAGE | 2024

This front yard in central Queens has adopted an austere palette of granite pavers and black rubber mulch that match the monochromatic color scheme of the semi-detached house and its dark windows. Only a couple of pink roses planted in the white urn at the tip of the V-shaped paver path add a bit of color, together with the weeds growing in the corners. Other than the gardens that have gone full-bleed, "wall-to-wall" Astroturf, or have been completely paved over, this is one of the most low-maintenance landscaping designs I have seen in the borough.

Fiery Front Garden

SOUTH OZONE PARK | 2024

At the opposite end of the matching home-and-garden color scheme is this fiery, red-and-orange front garden in southwestern Queens. Here, the homeowner has gone for maximum color impact by combining super-saturated hues with the various active textures of the house: English stucco, glazed brick, and ornate window trim. Also embellished with Hindu emblems, marigold garlands above the double door, and a *jhandi* flag in the corner of the white steel picket fence, it is clear that this small green space provides a transition from the secular streetscape to a sacred domestic realm.

Painted Curb Gardens

SOUTH OZONE PARK | 2024

Sometimes a garden is simply defined by a curb and a can, or two, of paint. This bright red curb with three courses of brick underlines a planting bed with various species of hydrangeas that spans the depth of the front yard. The facing page shows perhaps the most minimal garden in southwestern Queens, if not the entire borough, in which a few paver blocks define the corner of what was once a front yard but is now an extension of the sidewalk. Two concrete flower pots—painted white to match—add the botanical element and provide support to the edge-laid 8-inch paver blocks.

10934
109 30
109 34

Bent Garden Paths

SAINT ALBANS | 2024

The garden path is one of the most important elements in landscaping and determines how we experience various green spaces. At the mock-Tudor rowhouses of southeastern Queens, there is hardly a single straight path that traverses a front yard. Most are slightly curvilinear, but the two examples containing sharp bends featured here are among the more dramatic ones. In the above green-and-white painted garden, this path cuts through a loose assortment of pots and planter beds, recalling the obstacles in a pinball machine. To the right, a red thunderbolt.

114 22

SK's Cast-Off Garden

HOLLIS | 2024

After a hard day's work in the construction business, this Guyanese homeowner (known as "SK") likes to unwind in his front garden of cast-off building materials. He has fashioned a variety of stools and benches from tiles, blocks, and buckets for family and friends to join him. An L-shaped planter bed facing the neighbor and the street is capped with custom moldings (the corner pieces were cast using a plastic ashtray!). SK's daughter decided to highlight them, along with the bench, in a tropical turquoise—a popular color in this section of Queens, where many families are of Caribbean descent.

Sky Blue Banner Garden

SOUTH RICHMOND HILL | 2024

A bold, graphic design solution is used in this front garden to expand its perceived width to almost three times its actual size. By painting the scored path to the front steps and the corresponding section of driveway a brilliant sky blue, a tripartite composition—reminiscent of the Guatemalan flag—appears around the potted garden in the middle. Each of the twelve pots placed atop a grid of brick pavers contains a different plant species, making the garden look much more like an informal botanical exhibit than a natural green space. Scattered in between them is a loose bed of white gravel.

Pepperoni Garden Patio

MIDDLE VILLAGE | 2024

Here is another painted concrete garden made of loose bricks and potted plants, but in this case the pavers are round—like slices of pepperoni—and arranged symmetrically over a salmon-colored slab that matches the plastic terra cotta pots. It is fitting that the homeowner responsible for such a quirky, quasi-sculptural garden is named “Joy,” because that is exactly what her front yard “sparks,” to quote Marie Kondo’s popular catch phrase. Middle Village will never be the same.

Punch-Out Paver Gardens

SOUTH OZONE PARK | 2024

Queens is burning!—at least at these patio gardens in the southwestern section of the borough with their fiery punch-out pavers. The one above that has several flower pots sprinkled about and a porch that is also "ablaze" with the same light orange paint belongs to a large Pakistani family. To the right is an even hotter red-and-yellow patio that is devoid of any living botanical specimens. The only "green" in this front yard space is provided by the synthetic ivy strips that are threaded into the chain-link fence to create a privacy screen next to the entry porch.

Pop Art Patio

SOUTH OZONE PARK | 2024

This painted patio with its grid of (almost) twelve pink dots introduces some sixties Pop Art style to the everyday streetscape of southwestern Queens. Floating like pink lily pads in a subdued pool of gray, or a bouquet of giant carnations, these large circles with their abstract pattern evoke something natural and spring-like. As in the previous red-and-yellow garden, this front yard is also devoid of natural plants but it does have a clear lighting strategy, with lanterns in the two front corners and a white globe lamppost approximately halfway between the driveway and the front porch.

Aqua Checkerboard

MASPETH | 2023

Gardens are not just spaces for flowers and plants—they also make provisions for leisure and play. But the game being played on an aqua-colored checkerboard in this front yard seems to be mainly visual, if not metaphysical. It seems unlikely that the homeowners would turn their backs to the street by sitting on the pair of crescent-shaped benches that are focused on the single hydrangea bush. (Patio furniture typically faces outwards.) Instead, what we have here is more of a garden scene that invites the casual passerby to take a seat—figuratively speaking, of course.

Red Desert Garden

SOUTH JAMAICA | 2024

This painted garden goes beyond most of the other bold-colored gardens in the borough to evoke a little of the sublime. The mixture of fear and awe often provoked by nature is recreated here by the red desert floor of cracked earth pavers that covers the entire front yard, including the driveway, but not the footpath. The most visceral moment occurs at the tree planter where the earth opens up into a jagged-shaped hole to allow the roots to breathe and receive water. Just behind are a Japanese-style lantern and a rock fountain where koi used to swim, before the local racoon came to visit.

Yellow Lava Garden

SAINT ALBANS | 2024

Even bolder than the previous entry is this front yard that spills out onto a sidewalk that is painted "traffic yellow" to match the driveway and footpath of this single-family home in southeastern Queens (see above and following spread). The crooked stone benches, tilting lampposts, and loose lawn ornaments all look like they might be floating on top of a river of molten lava. Creeping Phlox and Blue Star juniper skillfully conceal the edges of the Astroturf lawn at the entry piers, while purple hydrangea shrubs offer a nice complementary touch to the bright yellow paving.

The Sacred and The Profane

BAYSIDE
CORONA
JACKSON HEIGHTS
MALBA
MASPETH
MIDDLE VILLAGE
MURRAY HILL
QUEENSBORO HILL
RICHMOND HILL
SOUTH OZONE PARK
WHITESTONE

Shrubs and Woodland Shrines

MASPETH | CORONA | 2022 | 2023

Shrines to the Virgin Mary are by far the most common expressions of devotion in the "World's Borough." Most of these are made from small prefab concrete niches, as seen at the edge of the koi pond in the "Fountains" chapter (p. 99). The above figure in the hollow of a faux tree trunk evokes medieval times when hermits prayed in the woods—a surprising scene to behold on the urban streets of Corona! But the photo to the left shows an even more surprising makeshift shrine: a life-size angel hiding next to a bush at the edge of the sidewalk—a jump scare moment as I walked by with my dog!

Ascendant Garden Goddess

MURRAY HILL | 2019

Many Queens homeowners like to use Ancient Greek and Roman themes to reimagine their gardens. Standing in for the original pine tree that cast deep shadows across the front yard of this single-family home is now an ethereal statue of Flora, the Roman goddess of flowers and spring. Framed by the Euonymus hedge to the front garden, spiral topiary, and the original arches of the porch, she has a temple-like aura that is quite conspicuous on the suburban streets of northeastern Queens, to say nothing about her non-existent attire: a gossamer gown and a garland of roses.

Recumbent Garden Nymph

WHITESTONE | 2024

A more relaxed version of the previous classical garden theme can be found a few neighborhoods away in this front yard in Whitestone. A slightly recumbent garden nymph sits next to a seashell birdbath with small animals at her feet as a pair of shy girls bite their dresses nearby. If we embrace Greek mythology, it is possible that this natural spirit, responsible for the care of plants and animals, could one day be transformed into a tree, as, most famously, was Daphne. But for now, she seems quite content to frolic in the front garden of this single-family home in northeastern Queens.

Angela's Sculpture Garden

MALBA | 2024

This garden, which occupies the edges of a two-car driveway in northeastern Queens, is a mash-up of sacred and profane statues from around the world. Cherubs, dolphins, mermaids, alligators, and angels on one side of the driveway face the seductive statue of Orisha Ochun, the Yoruba goddess of freshwater and fertility, on the other—Western European myth mixing with West African religion. Fusing everything together is the equally eclectic mix of botanical specimens, including everything from conifers to caladiums—and the sound of two running fountains (facing page and overleaf).

ORISHA OCHUN

PSI

Front Yard Muses

BAYSIDE | MIDDLE VILLAGE | 2024

Rounded hedges and gold-painted flower pots fill up the front garden of this mock-Tudor rowhouse in Middle Village. The largest of these golden pots has the form of a female head, whose goddess-like calm spreads tranquility over the entire botanical display. To the left is a decidedly more abstract version of the goddess Flora than we saw a few pages back in Murray Hill—one that seems to be coordinated with the architecture in the background. The strong triangular theme of the modified Cape-style home is echoed in the eight-pointed star design of the pedestal/planter.

Driveway Buddha

MIDDLE VILLAGE | 2024

This raised stone plinth between the driveway and the walkway of a post-war rowhouse in Middle Village is perhaps the most succinct representation of the sacred and the profane that I have come across in all of the Queens gardens. A kitschy sculpture of two Caucasian children chatting on a bench is positioned behind a meditating Buddha statue sitting on the ground. Both are painted silver in an attempt to bring them together visually, and both sit before turquoise flower pots filled with a variety of pink flowers.

Saint Joseph Sidewalk Garden

MIDDLE VILLAGE | 2023

At the end of a quiet residential street in Middle Village, this "bricklayer's special" consists of a semi-circular planter box and a corner shrine dedicated to Saint Joseph. The two geometries meet in such a way that they imply a footpath—or elevated catwalk, if you will—along the top of the curving planter that would allow the Holy Father to take a stroll around the garden, past the petunias, English yew, and hydrangea. Elaborate brick-wall front gardens are common in Queens and speak to a long tradition of semi-religious landscaping that can sometimes be confused with nativity scenes.

Side Yard Buddha

RICHMOND HILL | 2024

A much larger bronze-plated Buddha is the centerpiece of this side yard in southwestern Queens. It is so large that it inspired its own viewing pavilion in the form of a classical-style marble gazebo with a golden dome. The giant Buddha was acquired in Queens, and the gazebo was shipped from China. Clustered around the meditating statue are several topiary balls, Autumn Joy sedum (the pink flowers), and a collection of garden ornaments, including a stone lantern in the shape of a pagoda. Along the perimeter of the lawn, various shrubs lead to a large Blue Atlas cedar at the front gate.

A

Lord Shiva Corner Garden

SOUTH OZONE PARK | 2024

This Hindu version of the previous garden features a statue of Lord Shiva sitting under a stainless steel shrine with a plexiglass roof. Needless to say, this structure was not imported from China, or India, but, in all likelihood, fabricated at one of the many Queens metal shops that specialize in these types of shiny structures. Among Shiva's many powers and roles he is the protector of all creatures, as illustrated here by the two large plastic reindeer lawn ornaments that walk towards him. Not quite the sacred bull (aka Nandi) that he normally rides, but a slimmer, pagan version that is available stateside.

Jairo's Romantic Garden

JACKSON HEIGHTS | 2023 | 2024

At Jairo's home in northwestern Queens, romantic garden scenes with classical motifs guide the visitor from the street to the back corner of the rear yard. The tour begins curbside at the lush front garden (above) with a three-maiden bronze fountain at the center. Concrete cherubs peer out from the wall of ivy covering the central windows of the first floor. The breezy side yard facing north has several seating arrangements and a cluster of urns around a bust of Caesar (p. 196). More classical statues are sprinkled throughout the rear yard among chairs and recliners and overhead rose vines (right).

Chinese American Cooking Pavilion

QUEENSBORO HILL | 2024

Originally conceived as watchtowers during the period of the Warring States in Ancient China, the function of Chinese pavilions shifted towards the aesthetic, philosophical, and religious during the more peaceful times that followed. Wealthy homeowners incorporated them into their gardens as sheltered viewing structures and status symbols. Continuing the tradition in modern-day Queens, this well-to-do Chinese homeowner has maintained part of the original aesthetic function but also introduced a more American-style outdoor cooking component, complemented with folding lawn chairs.

All God's Creatures

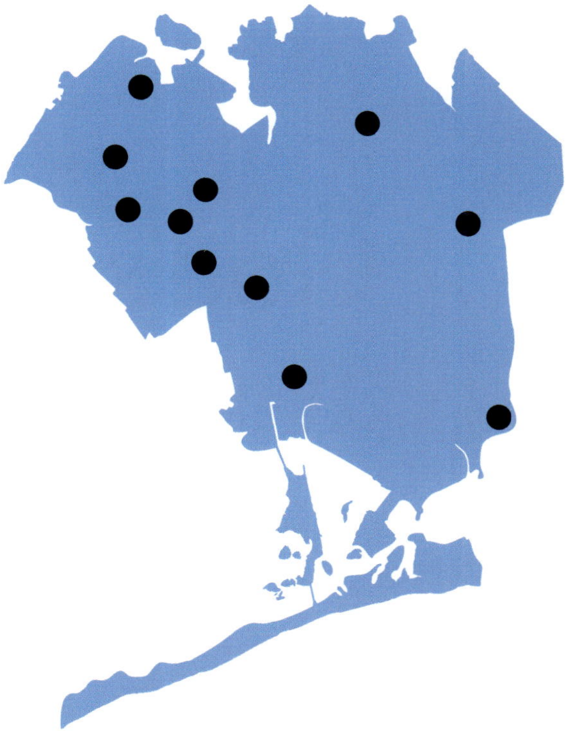

ASTORIA HEIGHTS
AUBURNDALE
GLENDALE
MASPETH
MIDDLE VILLAGE
QUEENS VILLAGE
REGO PARK
RICHMOND HILL
ROSEDALE
SOUTH OZONE PARK
SUNNYSIDE

Suburban Lions

SOUTH OZONE PARK | ROSEDALE | 2018 | 2019

Following in the tradition of surprising garden creatures that spans back to the Italian Renaissance and the infamous "Monster Park" at Bomarzo, the enormous front lawn ornament above is found in the southeastern neighborhood of Rosedale. A fiberglass lion about twice the size of the largest guard dog you will ever encounter will scare the bejesus out of you if you walk by unsuspectingly. To the left is a more regal expression of the lion ornament—in the British tradition—atop a stone post marking the corner of a garden (note the two-inch strip of grass between the pavers).

Elephants and Giraffes

QUEENS VILLAGE | RICHMOND HILL | 2024

Painted elephant finials on top of gates are common throughout southern Queens, especially in the South Asian neighborhoods, but elephant sculptures the size of gates in realistic gray tones are a rare find. The one to the right in Manni's front garden appears even bigger, given the small patio it resides in and the fact that this is filled with urns, raised planting beds, and a defunct triple-tier fountain. At Shika's garden in Queens Village (above), a more modestly scaled yellow giraffe pokes out between pink hydrangeas and hibiscus plants, next to the birdbath.

Painted Deer Gardens

MASPETH | ASTORIA HEIGHTS | GLENDALE | 2023 | 2024

Lawn ornaments in Queens can sometimes be "horses of a different color" or, in this case, deer. They are often painted in idiosyncratic ways that go beyond naturalistic representation. The above pair are covered in black flecks and have menacing green-and-white eyeballs, while the fawn to the left is covered in white blotches to match the adjacent pot of impatiens. The following spread shows a moment of magic realism at a typical row of attached houses in Glendale: two deer, one blue and one green, rest casually on a strip of Astroturf between the driveway (also Astroturfed) and the footpath.

8629

Shady Apes

SUNNYSIDE | AUBURNDALE | 2024

Mixing nature and legend into fantastical scenes is a time-honored tradition in gardens. Bigfoot (aka Sasquatch) figures are among the many mythical garden statues that one can purchase to insert an element of "the wild" into one's green space. But the curious thing about the Bigfoot in Auburndale (above) is that he is hiding the trunk of the Japanese maple, making the small tree look more like an haute couture feathered overcoat that he is parading down the runway than a hiding place in the wild. To the left, a large Sasquatch "peeking tree" statue in Sunnyside seeks to surprise passersby.

Squirrel Garden

REGO PARK | 2023

Of course, not all animal garden ornaments are intended to surprise, or scare, as in the previous lion and Bigfoot examples. In most cases, they are simply meant to cast the spell of Arcadia. Deer, rabbits, and donkeys are the animals usually chosen to evoke pastoral beauty within the quasi-urban conditions of present-day Queens. But in this duplex garden, the theme is inspired by local fauna. Squirrels are found in the planter beds and flower pots and climbing up the entry lamppost. One only wonders what their living counterparts think as they observe from the surrounding trees.

DON'T LEAVE
THE PACKAGE
WITHOUT
PRESSING
THE DOORBELL

Front Yard Safari

MIDDLE VILLAGE | 2024

At these brick row houses with large front yard setbacks and no driveways there is plenty of space to elaborate garden scenes. Most have kept the original grassy slope or built stepped planters for topiary and flowering shrubs, but at the house above a whole safari-like scene has been created under the canopies of various small trees. This open-air diorama of large reptiles and menacing felines is what one walks through on the way to the front door—garden as gauntlet, if you will. On a high wall up against the house is one last lion, perched over the city bins—recycle at your own risk!

Afterword

Rafael Herrin-Ferri

Four years ago, I was writing the foreword to my first book, *All the Queens Houses*, to tell the story of how I fell in love with the vernacular architecture of my home borough of Queens. Today I am writing the next chapter of that "love story," about the vernacular green spaces of Queens. This is not a story about Flushing Meadows Park—although it warrants many—or the great public parks in the borough such as Forest Park or Kissena, or even the community gardens sprinkled throughout, but instead of the private gardens that accompany the everyday houses of the "World's Borough."

As we have seen in the pages throughout the book, these gardens are for the most part street-facing, at the front or side of the house. Not surprisingly, some people have asked why more back gardens aren't included in the book. The answer is two-fold: first, the architecture of Queens houses typically favors the front for garden spaces (to the rear are service alleys with garages and laundry lines, back yards for basketball and barbecuing, small lawns to let the dogs loose in, etc.), and second, gardens are in large part an expression of the homeowners' personality, culture, and wealth, and in Queens—as in much of the rest of the world—these are proudly put on display.

In the 1920s, when Queens was developing into a suburban alternative to the most populous urbanized area in the world (Manhattan), much of its appeal lay in the opportunity to own a house and tend a garden. For this reason, many of the promotional materials advertised the newly built housing stock with pastoral references such as "single cottages" or "country homes," each with their respective "cottage gardens" (simple flower and vegetable gardens). Also promoting the idea of a country lifestyle were the borough's new neighborhood names: Forest Hills Gardens, Sunnyside Gardens, Kew Gardens (named after London's royal botanical garden), followed by many others with references to domesticated nature and green space: Rego Park, Glen Oaks, and Fresh Meadows, to name a few.

As I thought about Queens in this new, "greener" light, I embarked on another block-by-block photo survey of the "World's Borough," where my focus was not on housing but more on the specific garden trends of the vernacular, as opposed to the comprehensive, geographic portrait of all the neighborhoods that was the focus of the first book. And now that the Covid pandemic was over, I was able to converse with many homeowners face to face and get a deeper understanding of their gardens.

After meeting Lena on her porch in Ozone Park, I was finally able to make the connection between color and Hinduism. I had a vague notion from the first housing survey that these were linked when I noticed that the followers of the Indian guru Sri Chinmoy had painted their houses and businesses in Jamaica Hills light blue, but it was only after she explained that the bright red color of her porch was a tribute to the monkey-face deity Lord Hanuman—and I peeped his red banner in the bundle of jhandi flags—that the connection was clear (p. 147).

At the opposite end of Queens, in Whitestone, I came across the most impressive work of front yard folk art in the borough: "Salvatore's Sea Shell Extravaganza," (pp. 108–111). Like Sabato "Simon" Rodia, of Watts Towers fame in Los Angeles, Salvatore is also an Italian immigrant who laid tiles for a living and then built a highly idiosyncratic structure on his property. After speaking with him for a while, I was pleasantly surprised to learn that the shells he covers his two large fountains with are collected at the same New York beach I go to every summer with family and friends: Long Beach.

After dropping a third letter of interest in their mailbox, I was finally invited to tour Mr. & Mrs. Tom's pristine garden in Richmond Hill. Even though the main attraction is a spiritually charged centerpiece consisting of a large bronze Chinese Buddha and a golden-dome gazebo, the touching anecdote I think back to involved adoring poems printed on placards and placed between plants that ultimately gave the garden a more loving family vibe. "If we had a flower for each time we thought of our mother, we could walk in our garden forever," read one near the rear fence.

At times, Queens can feel like one giant Victorian garden—with a bunch of cars, roads, and houses thrown into the mix. The global mash-up of garden styles one experiences when walking the neighborhoods recalls the various "exotic" gardens of English estates such as Biddulph Grange or Alton Towers, but without the imperialistic undertones. The "exotic" plant specimens that fill these famous gardens were collected on high-profile expeditions and brought home in Wardian cases (beautiful glass containers that look like mini greenhouses), whereas the "exotic" plants and vegetables that fill contemporary Queens gardens are brought in under the radar—in plastic suitcases most likely—by the gardener's family and friends.

I have not attempted to count the number of species in Queens, but have been impressed by the diversity of plants, flowers, and vegetables that exist here.

The makeshift methods used by the immigrant population to grow food from their native countries never cease to amaze me. The Chinese are the masters of this. Their vegetable gardens are like DIY versions of victory gardens (gardens created during both world wars to reduce dependency on commercial food sources and ensure adequate food supplies for troops). As we have seen in the previous pages, these often have the aesthetics of "survival." By repurposing metal tubing, brightly-colored plastic containers, and other random objects, they create uncanny garden structures that come right up to the property line, or even hang over it at times.

But as impressed as I was with these Chinese vegetable gardens, and the diversity of plant species that exist throughout the borough, what really hit home was the diversity of garden types: flower gardens followed by sculpture gardens followed by painted gardens, and so on. Perhaps I shouldn't have been surprised, having already surveyed the borough once before, but it was very uplifting to see the multicultural and idiosyncratic character of Queens shining through its private green spaces as it does with its colorful façades. I hope this book will inspire us to reconsider the practice of everyday gardening as an integral part of the urban landscape—an art form that reminds us we are all creatures of God, who need a connection to nature.

Jackson Heights, New York
July 2025

Christopher Thacker, *The History of Gardens*. (University of California Press: Berkeley, 1979)

Gabrielle van Zuylen, *Paradise on Earth: The Gardens of Western Europe.* (Abrams: New York, 1995)

Jamie M. Allen and Sarah Anne McNear, *The Photographer in the Garden.* (Aperture: New York, 2018)

The English Garden. (Phaidon Press: London, 2008)

China: Art of Living/ Art of Surviving. (Fundació Joan Miró: Barcelona, 1995)

Acknowledgements

First and foremost, I would like to thank all the Queens gardeners who share their private green spaces with the public-at-large. This book is a tribute to the beauty, culture, and personality you bring to the "World's Borough." I would like to acknowledge the following gardeners for providing special access to their green spaces and sharing the stories behind them: Shika from Queens Village, Wazir from Laurelton, Steve and Joy from Middle Village, Feng and her friendly neighbor Suying from Murray Hill (thanks for the cherry tomatoes!), Shalini from South Ozone Park, Puja from Bellerose, Angela from Malba, Manni from Richmond Hill, Steven and Linda from Queensboro Hill (thanks for the winter melon!), Muhammed from South Jamaica, Melissa from Richmond Hill, Mike from Little Neck, Lena from Ozone Park, Andy from Richmond Hill (thanks for the ladder and umbrella!), Martha and Josephine from Elmhurst, Salvatore from Whitestone, Anthony from Hillcrest, and Jairo from Jackson Heights.

A very special thanks to NYBG botanist Jeffrey Ye for welcoming me into his sunken urban oasis (p. 65) a couple of years ago and helping identify many of the plant species in the book. Thanks to Lynnette Widder for her wonderful introductory essay and deep engagement on the subject of urban gardening. She and I would both like to thank her student Victoria Reshetnikov, for a highly creative project involving the World's Fair at Flushing Meadows Park, which helped connect us for this book.

As always, I would like to thank my parents for all their interest and encouragement, and my father specifically for his feedback on the text and making sure the language is accessible. I would also like to thank my uncle, the Spanish painter Antonio Ferri, who exposed me to the beauty of urban gardens at a young age—gracias Tio! And thanks to my wife and daughter for all their support during this second book and also for creating a virtual greenhouse of houseplants in our apartment that was a constant source of inspiration.

Finally, I would like to acknowledge that this publication was made possible (in part) with public funds from the Queens Arts Fund, a re-grant program supported by New York City Department of Cultural Affairs in partnership with the City Council and administered by the New York Foundation for the Arts. Thank you NYFA!

Imprint

© 2026 by jovis Verlag
An imprint of Walter de Gruyter GmbH, Berlin/Boston
Photographs, texts, and maps by kind permission of Rafael Herrin-Ferri.

All rights reserved.

Cover image: "Sidewalk Vegetable Pergola," 2023. Photograph by Rafael Herrin-Ferri.
Table of Contents image: "Defiance: The Lion King of Astoria," 2022. Photograph by Rafael Herrin-Ferri.
Introduction essay image: "Pastoral scene at Winfield, on the road from Long Island City to Flushing." The Miriam and Ira D. Wallach Division of Art, Prints and Photographs: Picture Collection, The New York Public Library.
Acknowledgements image: "Angel of Gratitude," 2023. Photograph by Rafael Herrin-Ferri.

Proofreading: Rupert Hebblethwaite, Vienna
Cover and design concept: Susanne Rösler, Berlin
Typesetting: Rafael Herrin-Ferri, New York
Lithography: Bild1Druck, Berlin
Printed: Graspo Cz, a. s., Zlín

For questions about the General Product Safety Regulation please contact productsafety@degruyterbrill.com.

Bibliographic information published by the Deutsche Nationalbibliothek
The Deutsche Nationalbibliothek lists this publication in the Deutsche Nationalbibliografie; detailed bibliographic data are available on the Internet at http://dnb.d-nb.de

jovis Verlag
Genthiner Straße 13
10785 Berlin

www.jovis.de

jovis books are available worldwide in select bookstores. Please contact your nearest bookseller or visit www.jovis.de for information concerning your local distribution.

ISBN 978-3-98612-243-0 (softcover)